THE HEART OF A
DISCIPLEMAKER

THE HEART OF A DISCIPLEMAKER

Building a Lasting Legacy Through
Authentic Relationships

Tim LaFleur

Published by Replicate Resources, Hendersonville, Tennessee.

ISBN-13: 978-1545293157 (Replicate Resources)
ISBN-10: 1545293155

Library of Congress Cataloging-in-Publication Data.

Printed in the United States of America.

To order additional copies of this resource, write to the following:
Replicate Ministries
3031 Long Hollow Pike
Hendersonville, TN 37075

Or e-mail info@replicate.org, or order online at www.amazon.com.

Acknowledgments

This book is the result of the hard work and help of many, and I am grateful for all who contributed.

For my children, Matt, Bre, Jonathan, and Elisabeth, and for their families, who are a blessing from God and are faithfully following after Christ.

For my former students from the Nicholls State University BCM, with whom it has been my joy to walk, find enrichment, and share what it means to follow Christ.

For Conrad and Carmen Beiber, who showed and shared with me how to follow Christ as a new believer.

For Robby Gallaty and the Replicate team, who challenged me to write this book.

For Hamilton Barber and my assistant, Robert Hutchison, who spent countless hours working with me to complete the final manuscript.

And most importantly, for my wife, Chris, the love of my life, who has been a faithful partner in ministry.

Contents

Foreword by Robby Gallaty

No one is more qualified to write a book on discipleship relationships than Tim LaFleur. Brother Tim—or Bro T, as the students he shepherded for so many years on the campus of Nicholls State University called him—epitomizes selfless service. My first introduction to Brother Tim was on March 16, 2004. I remember the date because the day before, I had met a girl named Kandi Ross for the first time, who would become my wife ten months later.

I had only been a believer for fifteen months when Tim invited me to speak for the Tuesday worship service at the BCM. My sermon that night, "A Recipe for Revival," was an interview for a summer camp opportunity in Glorieta, New Mexico. For years, Tim and his wife, Chris, coordinated the discipleship program for the college students who staffed the camp, called High Point.

The following week, Tim offered me the opportunity to spend the summer with him at Glorieta, investing in 130 college students, preaching once a week, and being discipled by him. I was facing a dilemma. The week before, I had been given an opportunity to preach five times a week up the East Coast with a summer camp called CentriKid. For an aspiring preacher, the thought of preaching five times a week compared to ten times the entire summer was alluring.

A DECISION THAT CHANGED MY LIFE

Providentially, I grabbed lunch with my friend Byron Townsend after church the Sunday before I had to make a decision. Byron was a seminary student at New Orleans, a former student at Nicholls State, and a disciple of Tim's. He said something to me that proved to be life changing afterward. "Robby," Byron said, "I know you think preaching multiple times a week this summer will make you a better preacher, but spending a summer with Tim will make you a better disciple. I believe a summer with Tim will change your life!"

I marinated on that one statement for days. Later that week, I accepted the position to be the camp pastor of High Point in Glorieta, New Mexico. It was one of the best decisions of my life. Brother Tim and I hit it off immediately. We were like two college buddies reunited after years apart. Immediately, we began meeting once a week for intentional discipleship. Tim taught me how to baptize someone (my first baptism was in the creek at Glorieta). He taught me how to organize a Bible study, how to organize sermons, and how to grill steaks, cook hamburgers, and play cards (no gambling was involved). I learned how to love and serve Kandi, who would become my wife after the summer, by watching Tim care for his wife, Chris. But Tim's investment was more than a weekly gathering.

People ask me often, "What was it like to spend a summer with Tim?" The late-night theological discussions over eschatology, identity in Christ, or assurance of salvation were memorable. But you know what was the most impactful? Watching him minister to others. His life-on-life approach taught me more than any theological lesson he shared. A discipleship principle I gleaned from Tim is that you can't expect from others what you aren't emulating yourself. Tim could speak with certainty on prayer because he and I were up at 6:00 a.m. every Tuesday and Thursday morning praying with students. Tim could give insights about the importance of having a daily quiet time with the Lord because he met with God every day in the Word. He could encourage others to labor in memorizing Scripture because he put in the time and effort to hide God's Word in his heart. (I believe he has most, if not all, the New Testament committed to memory.)

THE IMPORTANCE OF COMMUNITY

What Brother Tim taught me more than anything else is that relationships are not just important for the Christian life, but essential. Lone Ranger Christianity is an alien concept in the Bible. We cannot grow in isolation from others. Community is often synonymous with the word "fellowship," or *koinonia* in the Greek language. It is formed when men and women unite around a common interest, in this case, the gospel.

Author D. A. Carson wrote, "[The church] is made up of natural enemies. What binds us together is not common education, common race, common income levels, common politics, common nationality, common accents, common jobs, or anything else of that sort. Christians come together...because they have all been saved by Jesus Christ...They are a band of natural enemies who love one another for Jesus's sake."[i]

Remember, Jesus is not an isolated rabbi separated from history. The gospel of our Lord is interconnected with a chosen people, Israel. God promised to impact the world through a nation, a community. Additionally, Jesus started a disciplemaking movement through a community of twelve men. Christian relationships are distinctively different because Jesus has made us different.

Why do I bring this up? Disciplemaking happens through intentional, intimate relationships with other people. The commands of Christ are carried out with other believers. The Bible is replete with passages urging us to join in fellowship, and we are commanded to live out the "one anothers" with those around us. Here are a few of those commands:

- Love one another (John 13:34).
- Be in agreement with one another (Rom. 12:16).
- Accept one another (Rom. 15:7).
- Instruct one another (Rom. 15:14).
- Greet one another (Rom. 16:16).
- Serve one another (Gal. 5:13).
- Be kind and compassionate to one another (Eph. 4:32).
- Submit to one another out of reverence for Christ (Eph. 5:21).
- Admonish one another with all wisdom (Col. 3:16).
- Encourage one another, and build each other up (1 Thess. 5:11).
- Be hospitable to one another (1 Pet. 4:9).
- Confess your sins to one another, and pray for one another (James 5:16).

It's impossible to implement these words in isolation. Dietrich Bonhoeffer said it best: "Sin demands to have a man by himself. It withdraws him from the community. The more isolated a person is, the more destructive will be the power of sin over him."[ii] We are sharpened by other believers and strengthened in community. Some of the greatest life lessons I've learned have been from other people.

In *The Heart of a Disciplemaker*, Tim weaves scriptural principles with personal disciplemaking stories to teach life-changing truths. This book speaks to the heart of every disciple who desires to make disciples. You will find Tim's conversational writing style to be both accessible and inspiring at the same time. Don't just read this book. Pass it on to those you're investing in.

Introduction

"You've got to come to youth camp with me, Tim," Mike pleaded. "My grandmother is making me go, and it won't be any fun without you. Besides, there are always some good-looking girls there!" The last sentence was what roped me in. Little did I know the decision to go meet pretty girls at youth camp would lead to the greatest experience of my life: the moment I met my Savior, Jesus Christ. My encounter with the God of the universe changed the course of my life forever.

As an older teenager who grew up Roman Catholic, I was far from God. I was too busy doing all the things most teenagers did in my hometown instead of seeking a relationship with Him. When Mike's grandparents told him he was going to camp, hoping he might be saved, it was only natural that I would go with him.

But getting saved was the last thing on our minds as we headed out in his Volkswagen Beetle to a youth camp more than seventy miles away. On the way, we did what we always did. He smoked cigarettes, and I drank beer. As you can imagine, when we arrived, we stuck out like sore thumbs. It was only by the grace of God that we didn't get booted from camp the very first day.

When we got into the routine of camp, I discovered that my friend was right. There really were some good-looking girls there. But I noticed they were very different from the girls I knew. They seemed to love God in a deep, intentional way. I remember how confused I became. Although I knew a lot about God, I didn't have the same devotion to Him they seemed to have. They not only knew about God, but they claimed to have a relationship or friendship with Him.

As I observed these students, I began to want what they had—an authentic relationship with Christ. In fact, it seemed to be the strangest thing; all I wanted was to know God the way they did. They had such a walk and friendship with Him that I could see Jesus in them, and I became very attracted to the gospel.

Besides seeing Christ in them, I was also moved by the Bible teaching and discussion. I began to realize that I was separated from God and was a sinner who needed a Savior. So at the end of one of the worship gatherings, after hearing the gospel, I bowed a knee to Jesus and asked Him to be my Lord and my Savior. I turned from my sin and put my faith and trust in Christ alone.

I'll never forget the sensation I had when I bowed my knee to the Lord Jesus. I felt that the weight of the world was taken off my shoulders, that I was a new person, and that God had forgiven my sin and made me clean.

One of the pastors there from Kentucky, Brother Godwin, shared something that has stuck with me to this day. He said, "Tim, the Christian life is either easy or impossible. It is impossible when you try to live it in your own strength, but it becomes more easy [his words] when you allow Christ to live His life in and through you."

PRESS
SPENT
from-Goodfight-
WORKOUT
2TM 2:1-7

Another one of the student pastors gave me a Bible and encouraged me to read and meditate on the parts he had highlighted to help me as a new believer.

As you might imagine, my newfound faith and relationship with Christ excited me. But there was one problem. I felt all alone. Before going to the student camp, I had never met a born-again believer. My family was lost, my friends were lost, and as far as I knew, my teachers were lost. I had no one to help and encourage me to grow in my walk with Christ.

In my hometown, I knew about two churches: the Catholic church I had gone to my whole life and the First Baptist church on the other side of town.

I heard that the Baptist church taught the Bible, so I started attending services there. When I visited, I was overcome by the love and acceptance the members of that congregation extended to me. They accepted me as I was. As I became more involved in the church, I came to the realization that it wasn't solely an institution to attend, but it was a family to be part of. I was eager to obey God, and when I discovered that God expected new believers to follow Him in baptism, I decided to get baptized.

My mother, who was Catholic in name only, became very angry with me and my decision to follow Christ. In fact, because I got baptized, she put me out of our house. She asked, "Are you becoming a member of that cult?" and said I'd have to leave home at once.

I didn't know where to go or what to do, but my Sunday school teacher allowed me to live with him and his family. Conrad and Carmen, along with their newborn son, Brian, lived in a two-bedroom home on his rice farm. It was still summer at the time, and Conrad allowed me to work alongside him on his farm. We were together almost all the time. He taught me how to drive a tractor, use a shovel, and so much more.

But the most significant thing Conrad did that summer was invest his life in mine. He helped to nurture me as a new believer, and I was never the same—all because this rice farmer took the time to invest in my life. I learned to pray because he prayed with me. I learned to read the Bible because he did. I learned to memorize Scripture because it was a discipline in his life. I learned to share my faith because I saw him show and share the love of Christ with everyone. I learned to honor God with my finances because I saw him give to the church and to those in need.

It was life-on-life discipleship. Conrad modeled what it looked like to follow Christ, and I followed his example. He was always ready and willing to answer my questions and hear my heart.

It is hard to say where I would be without Conrad's influence in my life. I can't begin to imagine what my life would have looked like if God hadn't brought this godly mentor to me.

I wanted to share my testimony with you about how I came to know Christ so you would know one of the reasons I am so passionate about making disciples. I am the product of disciplemaking. I wrote this book with several core convictions in mind that you should be aware of.

THE BIBLE IS THE WORD OF GOD

I believe that the Bible is the inspired, inerrant Word of God. It is God's truth without any mixture of error. It is the sole authority for our faith and should guide all that we are and all that we do in the kingdom. It is God's revelation to man about Himself and His plan of redemption through His Son, Jesus.

That being said, we don't measure the Bible by our experience; we measure our experience by the Bible. We don't measure God's Word through the lens of other books; we measure other books through the lens of the Bible.

When it comes to making disciples, the Bible should be the textbook. Sure, it's okay to use other books in the process. Outside resources can be helpful, but they never trump or overshadow the Bible.

The Bible is enough to equip believers for every good work. Paul said it this way: "All Scripture is inspired by God and is profitable for teaching, for rebuking, for correcting, for training in righteousness, so that the man of God may be complete, equipped for every good work" (2 Tim. 3:16–17).

THE GOSPEL

The gospel hinges upon three historical facts: the death, burial, and resurrection of Jesus the Nazarene. Paul also thought these three facts were the central tenets of the gospel: "For I passed on to you as most important what I also received: that Christ died for our sins according to the Scriptures, that He was buried, that He was raised on the third day according to the Scriptures" (1 Cor. 15:3–4).

Jesus Christ, fully God and fully man, became our sin bearer, was buried, and was raised to life. He is alive and offers His life to all who will repent of their sin and believe in Him.

What grace! All who have come to faith in Jesus Christ should show and share the gospel with everyone everywhere. Don't think about it as something that dropped in your lap for you to consume and hoard; *the gospel came to you on its way to someone else.* Those of us who have received the gospel should give it away.

MAKING DISCIPLES

Making disciples is the final command of Christ (Matt. 28:18–20) and should be the primary work of the local church. We should make disciples in the context of the local church and not separate or apart from it.

To make disciples, you must first be a disciple. A disciple is a learner and a follower. He or she is not only learning the truth about Christ; he or she is putting that truth into practice. So if you are not learning about Christ, if you are not following Him, and if you are not being obedient to Him, you cannot expect to lead others to learn, follow, and obey Christ.

I often say, "You can't lead folks on a journey you haven't been on." If you aren't following after Christ, it is impossible to model what it looks like to follow Him for those you invest in.

THE HOLY SPIRIT

If you are going to make disciples, you must be a disciple—learning, loving, obeying, and following after the Lord Jesus. It doesn't take long until you realize that following after Christ is an impossible task if you try to do it in your own strength and power.

Consider the demands:

"Love your enemies and pray for those who persecute you" (Matt. 5:44).

"Be perfect, therefore, as your heavenly Father is perfect" (Matt. 5:48).

"For it is written, be holy, because I am holy" (1 Pet. 1:16).

"Don't worry about anything, but in everything, through prayer and petition with thanksgiving, let your requests be made known to God" (Phil. 4:6).

J. Oswald Saunders helped us too: "Is God so unreasonable as to make impossible demands on us and then hold us responsible for our failures? Our conscious spiritual inadequacy underlines our need for a partner who has adequate spiritual resources from which we can draw."[iii]

God has provided this unseen partner in the presence and power of the Holy Spirit. The third person of the Godhead indwells His disciples and empowers their walk and witness. He will provide all the resources we need to follow Christ and help others to follow Him as well.

GOSPEL-CENTERED RELATIONSHIPS

Years of experience have led me to believe that the process of making disciples occurs best in gender-specific groups of three to five people meeting for the purpose of spiritual growth and accountability. In this environment, gospel-centered relationships grow and flourish.

Gospel-centered relationships are formed as we live in surrender to Christ and the gospel. These relationships with others don't happen by accident; they must be intentional. We must always be giving one another permission to hold each other accountable, encourage one another, and persevere in the journey to be all that we can be for Christ!

This book is not so much about a *model* or a *method* to make disciples; it is about the *manner* in which we make disciples. It will focus on the heart and the character of those who invest in others: the kinds of character qualities that will encourage others to follow Christ through meaningful, dynamic, gospel-centered relationships.

1

Cultivating a Shepherd's Heart

Dr. Lynn Anderson helps us understand the necessity of being among the people we minister to in his book *They Smell like Sheep*. If I presented you with two different shepherds and asked you to choose which of them did his job better, you'd likely choose the one who smelled most like sheep. That shepherd would have spent his days and nights among them. He would know the different sheep's personalities. He'd understand what kind of pitfalls they were prone to.[iv]

Paul made the same kind of case for how to care for people in 1 Thessalonians 2. In that chapter, he remembered the way he and his coworkers lived with and cared for new believers in Thessalonica. Paul the preacher became Paul the shepherd by nurturing and helping them grow deep in their newfound faith.

As we will discover, this chapter in 1 Thessalonians explained that an effective disciplemaker ought to have the heart of a shepherd. Paul explained in detail what he and his coworkers felt and experienced, the things he did as a shepherd, and how the new believers responded. It is a shining example of how we ought to not only proclaim the gospel with our lips but also model the gospel by our manner of life.

We can have meaningful gospel-centered relationships as we make disciples when we apply these key principles taken from 1 Thessalonians 2.

1. ENTRUST THE GOSPEL IN SPITE OF ADVERSITY.

For you yourselves know, brothers, that our visit with you was not without result. On the contrary, after we had previously suffered, and we were treated outrageously in Philippi, as you know, we were emboldened by our God to speak the gospel of God to you in spite of great opposition. For our exhortation didn't come from error or impurity or an intent to deceive. (1 Thess. 2:1–3)

Paul and his coworkers endured much hardship, like beatings with rods and imprisonment, but still remained faithful (see Acts 16). It would have been easy to throw in the towel, but instead, they grew bolder in their efforts to share the gospel!

If you commit to sharing Christ and making disciples, it will cost you something and will require sacrifice at some level. You may not be beaten or imprisoned, but it will cost you things like time, money, convenience, and peace of mind at the very least. As someone has said, "Ministry that costs nothing accomplishes nothing."

When we share the gospel "in spite of great opposition," it becomes clear that we are pouring ourselves into the lives of others with the right motives, not with "impurity or an intent to deceive."

I'll never forget the first time I met Ramon Hernandez. He stood about six feet tall, and he had a rugged build and jet-black hair. Ramon looked more like a wilderness outfitter than a missionary. Little did I know that would begin a rich gospel-centered relationship that would span the course of more than twenty years.

My team and I had driven to Texas from Louisiana the day before and met Ramon for breakfast. Ramon then helped us cross the border into Mexico and navigate our way through the military checkpoints.

I traveled with Pastor Ramon as we crossed the border and were on our way to the interior of Mexico. Although he spoke broken English, we were able to communicate. As we traveled, we talked about his heart for church planting and missions. It became obvious that Pastor Ramon was the real deal: the churches in his network were not only thriving but planting other churches!

He told us how he and his mission teams had suffered persecution for the sake of the gospel. They had been abused, mistreated, stoned, and driven out of town for their faith. Yet, in spite of the persecution, the churches they planted continued to grow and flourish. They were faithful to make disciples even in the midst of adversity.

Jesus knows that His followers will face opposition and tough times. But some of the greatest comforts to us are His words found in the Great Commission in Matthew 28. As we are making disciples, Jesus promised, "I am with you always, to the end of the age" (Matt. 28:20).

2. ENTRUST THE GOSPEL WITH INTEGRITY.

For our exhortation didn't come from error or impurity or an intent to deceive. Instead, just as we have been approved by God to be entrusted with the gospel, so we speak, not to please men, but rather God, who examines our hearts. For we never used flattering speech, as you know, or had greedy motives—God is our witness—and we didn't seek glory from people, either from you or from others. (1 Thess. 2:3–6)

Notice the integrity, godly character, and sincerity with which Paul and his partners ministered to these new believers. More than anything else, their desire was to please God, which they proved by their godly character and conduct. Paul and his ministry partners were not seeking the applause of men but the approval of God!

For twenty years, I had the privilege of doing campus-based ministry in south Louisiana. I was the Baptist Collegiate ministry director on the campus of Nicholls State University, where I worked with many college students who wanted to make a difference for the kingdom.

One such student was a young woman named Tara. Tara was one of many students who helped lay a foundation for the kind of ministry we desired to have on campus. Her manner of life was beyond reproach: she walked with God, shared her faith, mentored other young women, and had a gospel witness in the marching band.

Tara now leads a ministry in Houma, Louisiana, where she brings hope by sharing the light and life of Jesus with urban youth.

We must always remember to serve with integrity, no matter where we find ourselves. Serve God with a pure heart, for He is a God who sees past our actions into our motives. Make your life all about bringing glory to God, the only One worthy of all praise and glory.

3. ENTRUST THE GOSPEL IN LOVE.

> Although we could have been a burden as Christ's apostles, instead we were gentle among you, as a nursing mother nurtures her own children. We cared so much for you that we were pleased to share with you not only the gospel of God but also our own lives, because you had become dear to us. (1 Thess. 2:7–8)

Paul and his coworkers loved these people! In his book *Reaching the Next Level*, Pete Charpentier wrote, "As a mother who compassionately cares for her children, Paul made every effort to be gentle with these new believers."[v]

They didn't only share the gospel but also their very lives. Because these new believers had become very dear to them, it was Paul's joy to share every piece of himself. Making disciples is what we do; love is why we do it.

The motivation for gospel work must be the love of Christ! As Paul says in 2 Corinthians, "For Christ's love compels us, since we have reached this conclusion: If One died for all, then all died" (2 Cor. 5:14).

Frank Horton was a trusted counselor, mentor, confidant, and close personal friend to students on the campus of Louisiana State University. He influenced and impacted many students for Christ, including me.

Mr. Horton (as I called him) was not a gifted preacher or teacher; in fact, there was nothing outstanding or out of the ordinary that would attract you to him. What stood out about him was how he loved his students. He was patient and long-suffering, and he loved students in spite of their flaws. Frank Horton affected my life in a profound way and became the model that I have patterned my life and ministry after.

Mr. Horton lived out Jesus's words in John 13:34–35, where Jesus said, "I give you a new command: Love one another. Just as I have loved you, you must also love one another. By this all people will know that you are My disciples, if you have love for one another."

The motive for every gospel-centered relationship must be love. It is love for God, but we express it outwardly and soak every Christ-centered relationship in it. Paul explained it to Timothy like this: "Now the goal of our instruction is love that comes from a pure heart, a good conscience, and a sincere faith" (1 Tim. 1:5).

4. ENTRUST THE GOSPEL FIRMLY.

As you know, like a father with his own children, we encouraged, comforted, and implored each one of you to walk worthy of God, who calls you into His own kingdom and glory. (1 Thess. 2:11–12)

There are times when we must nurture new believers gently, but there are other times when we must exhort and encourage them with firmness. Notice the contrast between the gentleness of a nursing mother and the firmness of a father. Paul and his coworkers used both. They ministered with strength and gentleness. The seasoned disciplemaker knows when to be strong and when to be gentle.

Brandon was my ministry intern and a student pastor for a local church from 2002 to 2003. From the beginning, Brandon was a great student of the Bible and showed signs of being a gifted teacher, but he needed to grow as a servant leader.

After an event that his church sponsored, I noticed that Brandon had gone home early, leaving the cleanup to his pastor and me. So I pulled him aside, and we discussed servanthood and servant leadership. Brandon thanked me for the fatherly talking-to and over time made the adjustments needed to become a true servant leader. Brandon and his wife, Mindy, are now missionaries in Eastern Europe.

As you share your life with others, don't be afraid to be direct with those you disciple and mentor. Sometimes tough love is required.

5. ENTRUST THE GOSPEL WITH THANKSGIVING.

> This is why we constantly thank God, because when you received the message about God that you heard from us, you welcomed it not as a human message, but as it truly is, the message of God, which also works effectively in you believers. For you, brothers, became imitators of God's churches in Christ Jesus that are in Judea, since you have also suffered the same things from people of your own country, just as they did from the Jews. (1 Thess. 2:13–14)

As Paul and his coworkers invested in the believers of Thessalonica, it was obvious that God was doing something special. These believers were making spiritual progress, and for that Paul and his team were grateful to God.

You and I must be faithful to share the gospel. We must also be thankful for the privilege God gives us to do ministry, especially as He works through us to meet the needs of others for His glory.

I met Pete on a Sunday night at the church where I was pastoring. His parents forced him and his brothers to come to church. As you can imagine, they had bad attitudes and nothing good to say, and they were generally disinterested.

As I began to develop a relationship with Pete and his brothers, I really enjoyed being around them. I went to eat lunch with them at school, visited with them in their home, and hung out with them during youth group. After some time, I had the wonderful privilege of leading Pete to faith in Christ and then discipling him. Pete showed promise of growth and transformation from the beginning. He always wanted to talk about God and His Word, loved to serve others, and had a desire to share his faith with his friends in school. It was obvious that God was doing something special in his life.

As he grew in his faith, what set him apart from his peers was his faithfulness to God. He was faithful even when his friends made fun of him. They thought Pete was weird because he prayed before meals, carried his Bible along with his school textbooks, and would share a "word fitly spoken" with all who would listen.

Pete's senior year of high school was quite different. Because he had modeled faithfulness and authenticity before his friends, they began to seek him out for advice and counsel. I prayed at Pete's graduation and was so encouraged when many of his friends and classmates shared about the difference he had made in their lives.

Pete's faithfulness is the hallmark of his ministry today. Dr. Charpentier is a pastor and seminary professor in the Southwest. Because of his faithfulness, many are being impacted by the gospel, resulting in thanksgiving to God!

6. ENTRUST THE GOSPEL WITH COURAGE.

For you, brothers, became imitators of God's churches in Christ Jesus that are in Judea, since you have also suffered the same things from people of your own country, just as they did from the Jews. (1 Thess. 2:14)

These new believers were experiencing some of the same opposition that Paul and his team were facing, yet they served Christ without fear.

Persecution helped these believers in at least two ways.

First, it helped serve as a catalyst for prayer. Paul's great desire was for these believers; he longed for them. And because he had them in his heart and on his mind, he constantly lifted them up in prayer!

The persecution also proved the reality of their faith. *Persecution will always prove the authenticity of a believer's faith.* Warren Wiersbe wrote, "The church persecuted, becomes the church pure; while the church patronized becomes the church polluted!"[vi]

7. ENTRUST THE GOSPEL WITH JOY.

For who is our hope or joy or crown of boasting
in the presence of our Lord Jesus at His coming?

Is it not you? For you are our glory and joy! (1 Thess. 2:19–20).

Paul and the team found great joy in their relationship with these new believers in Thessalonica. Because they had become a part of God's forever family, they knew these relationships would be lasting ones. Paul expressed how this made him feel when he wrote, "You are our glory and joy!"

Through the years of ministry, God has enriched my life by allowing me to invest in many young men and women who are either in vocational ministry, are married to someone in vocational ministry, or are serving God in their local churches. It is such a joy to watch them grow, see them develop, and cheer them on as they serve the Lord Jesus and further the gospel!

The most meaningful relationships I have experienced as a believer have been in the context of disciplemaking relationships. When they call for encouragement or advice, share a victory or challenge, or need insight because of some crisis, it seems that we pick up right where we've left off even though we may not have seen or talked to each other in some time. These relationships are unending.

As you invest in others and cultivate gospel-centered relationships, you will find the greatest joy you've ever known.

2

Character Counts

Many years ago, Johnny challenged our D-group by saying, "Only three things are eternal: God, His Word, and the souls of men. Invest in these things!" Right then, I knelt in prayer and asked God to help me invest in the things that are eternal and not the things that will fade.

Encouraging one another to focus on what matters is one of the reasons discipleship groups produce such rich and growing gospel-centered relationships. The disciplemaker has the chance to talk about God and His Word so those in his or her group can know what it means to follow Him.

D-groups produce strong gospel-centered relationships because they're based on accountability. A

D-group member can ask the other members questions like these:

- "Are you dying to self and the self-life?"
- "Are you dealing with the indwelling sin in your life?"
- "Are you loving your spouse and children the way Christ would?"
- "Are you sharing the love of Christ with your friends and your coworkers?"
- "Are you spending time with God and His Word?"

Furthermore, trust and transparency grow as friendships develop and as you walk together. You will develop the freedom to share with each other, the desire to encourage each other, and the feeling of responsibility for one another. As members of the group fill their hearts and minds with the Word of God and pray for one another daily, they will share in the joy of being disciples of Christ.

Disciplemakers empower others to form deep relationships that center around Christ. But with that privilege comes great responsibility! They must have the "right stuff" if they're going to make disciples who make disciples.

You must have seven essential qualities if you wish to make disciples who make disciples.

1. A HEART FOR GOD

Having a heart for God means desiring to know Him in a deep, intimate way and to make Him known. Notice what Jesus said in Matthew's Gospel: "'Love the Lord your God with all your heart, with all your soul, and with all your mind. This is the greatest and most important command'" (Matt. 22:37–38).

Disciplemakers ought to have a desire to love God with all their hearts, souls, and minds. Jesus said this is the "greatest and most important command."

My friend Chris Adsit, before writing his book *Personal Disciplemaking*, surveyed more than five hundred disciplemakers from all over the world. In these interviews, he asked them what the most important qualities for making disciples were. More than one-third ranked having a heart for God as number one, and most ranked this quality in the top three.[vii] Sometimes, though, a heart for God gets developed in mysterious ways.

Jesse and his brothers were members of a garage band named Ola-Wyne in the early eighties. They had long hair and the rebellious attitude that went along with it. They were good kids but were far from God.

While serving as a pastor of a small church on the bayou in south Louisiana, I had the privilege of leading Jesse to faith in Christ and discipling him.

After Jesse came to the Lord and began a discipleship relationship, something shifted in him. Soon, whenever anyone looked at him, the first thing they noticed was his love for and devotion to God. On many occasions when I went to visit with his family, I found Jesse in the cane fields spending time alone with God, studying His Word, worshiping Him, and interceding in prayer for his family and friends. Jesse proclaimed his devotion even when it wasn't popular, led many of his classmates to Christ, and stood for God no matter what the cost.

Jesse is now a pastor in south Louisiana and is investing in many others who need Christ. His love and devotion to the Lord Jesus and the gospel still characterize his ministry to this day.

Those used mightily by God to make disciples are those who have a heart for God and His Word.

2. LOVE FOR THOSE YOU DISCIPLE

You must cultivate not only a growing love relationship with Christ but also a love for those you disciple. Notice what Jesus said in Matthew 22:39: "The second [greatest command] is like it: Love your neighbor as yourself."

We are not only to have a love for God; we are to have a love for people. More than anything else, your disciples must know that you love them! As Peter said: "Above all, maintain an intense love for each other, since love covers a multitude of sins" (1 Pet. 4:8).

You must never look at your disciple as a "project." He or she is someone you are called to love!

Many have said throughout the years, "People don't care how much you know until they know how much you care."[viii]

Talk can be cheap. Prove your love by spending time with your disciples. You show them you care about them by cultivating real relationships with them. You then earn the right to speak into their lives because they realize you care for them and their families.

One of the first guys I discipled in campus ministry was a young man named Shawn. Shawn was a student who began to hang out at our campus ministry building, the Nicholls Baptist Student Union. As I got to know Shawn better, it became obvious that he lacked a man's influence in his life. His dad was absent from the home.

I began to invite Shawn to cookouts, outings, and events with our family. Before long, Shawn became one of the family. What was the difference that made the difference? The love of Christ! "I give you a new command," Jesus said. "Love one another. Just as I have loved you, you must also love one another. By this all people will know that you are My disciples, if you have love for one another" (John 13:34–35).

3. A GODLY LIFESTYLE

As a disciplemaker, you must not only profess Christ; you must live a life consistent with what you profess to believe. When writing to the Colossians, Paul said this was "so that you may walk worthy of the Lord, fully pleasing to Him, bearing fruit in every good work and growing in the knowledge of God" (Col. 1:10). It is every believer's job to walk worthy of the Lord.

This is especially true for those who make disciples. Not only are your disciples listening to what you say, but they are observing the way you live. Consider what Paul told the Thessalonians: "We cared so much for you that we were pleased to share with you not only the gospel of God but also our own lives, because you had become dear to us. For you remember our labor and hardship, brothers. Working night and day so that we would not burden any of you, we preached God's gospel to you" (1 Thess. 2:8–9).

Their witness had a maximum impact because they not only talked the talk but walked the walk! The believers at Thessalonica learned Christ through the examples of Paul, Timothy, and Silas. It's as my friend Bill Stafford says, "Your talk talks, and your walk talks. But your walk always talks louder than your talk talks."

4. FRIENDSHIP WITH YOUR DISCIPLES

One of the great byproducts of disciplemaking is the friendships I have forged through the years. This would be the overflow of really having a love for your disciples. As you really love the people you are investing in, it stands to reason that you would also grow as friends. My friend John Kelsey, who serves with the Navigators, goes as far as describing disciplemaking as "friendship with a vision." In D-groups, you not only cultivate disciples, but you also forge life-long friendships. Some of the greatest friendships I have ever known have been in the context of a D-group.

I'll never forget the first time I met Preston. He was a student who got involved in our campus ministry.

After getting to know Preston, I discovered he had grown up in church and served in one of the largest, most dynamic student ministries in the state. Although he knew the language of the church, over time it became clear Preston was far from God.

Several of the guys on our flag football team invited Preston to play, and he agreed. As he got acquainted with the guys, Preston soon realized that he didn't have something they had. He realized by observing their examples that what they had was an authentic relationship with Christ. Preston trusted Jesus as Savior and Lord and became a Christ follower.

When you invest your life in others, you should seek to develop friendships with them.

5. WILLINGNESS TO PRAY FOR YOUR DISCIPLES

E. M. Bounds said, "You can't rightly talk to men about God, until you first talk to God about men."[ix]

If you are partnering with the Holy Spirit to impact those you disciple, it stands to reason that you should pray for them. Trust God to do what only He can do to work in the lives of those you are investing in.

Jesus exemplified this in His ministry by praying for His disciples. John 17 recorded what may be the greatest prayer ever prayed. In that prayer, Jesus prayed primarily for His disciples:

> I have given them Your word. The world hated them because they are not of the world, as I am not of the world. I am not praying that You take them out of the world but that You protect them from the evil one. They are not of the world, as I am not of the world. Sanctify them by the truth; Your word is truth. As You sent Me into the world, I also have sent them into the world. I sanctify Myself for them, so they also may be sanctified by the truth. (John 17:14–19)

Paul also gave us a practical model of what it looks like to pray for our disciples. In fact, he prayed for the believers in almost every letter he wrote. Look at Paul's prayer for the believers in Ephesus:

This is why, since I heard about your faith in the Lord Jesus and your love for all the saints, I never stop giving thanks for you as I remember you in my prayers. I pray that the God of our Lord Jesus Christ, the glorious Father, would give you a spirit of wisdom and revelation in the knowledge of Him. I pray that the perception of your mind may be enlightened so you may know what is the hope of His calling, what are the glorious riches of His inheritance among the saints, and what is the immeasurable greatness of His power to us who believe, according to the working of His vast strength. (Eph. 1:15–19)

Paul not only shared who these believers were in Christ, but he prayed they would see the vast wealth they had in Him. He then prayed they could put what they knew into practice and that God would enable them to do it.

That would be my prayer for you: that you would be enlightened to all the qualities you possess in

Christ and that you would be equipped and empowered to make disciples.

6. PATIENCE

One of the fundamental principles of spiritual growth is that it takes time. I like what Paul said in 1 Corinthians 3:6: "I planted, Apollos watered, but God gave the growth." Paul and Apollos did their parts, but God is the one who gives the growth. Growth takes time!

There's an old story of a young seminarian who wanted to finish his coursework early so he could hurry to the mission field. He asked his professor, "Can I fit three years of study into two so that I can go the mission field?"

The wise professor responded, "You know, son, it takes God only six months to grow a squash, but it takes Him one hundred years to grow a magnificent oak. What do you want to be?"

The student replied, "I think I'll finish the complete course."[x]

It takes time for God to grow those you invest in. There will be obstacles, challenges, and struggles along the way. But as you journey together with those you invest in, God will be the one to conform them to the image of Christ in His own sovereign time.

When you disciple others, you must be steadfast, patient, and long-suffering, realizing that God gives the growth.

7. DESIRE TO LEARN

A disciple is, by definition, a learner. Someone who invests in others should be a lifelong learner so he or she continues to model a life that is rich and growing.

The first time I met Robby Gallaty was in the spring of 2004. Tony Merida suggested that I invite him to speak to our college students at our weekly worship gathering at the Baptist Collegiate Ministry (BCM). When Robby arrived, all eyes were on him. He was massive: six feet six and about 285 pounds. Honestly, he looked more like a professional football player than a guest speaker. But it was evident as he spoke that he had a zeal for God and an authentic experience with Jesus.

As I became better acquainted with Robby, I realized that he was passionate about knowing Christ and making Him known. He had an insatiable desire to learn and grow as a believer. As I got to know him, I became convinced he should help me with High Point, a discipleship ministry in Glorieta, New Mexico. We spent the next summer learning, growing, and journeying together.

Today, Dr. Robby Gallaty is the senior pastor at Long Hollow Baptist Church and still has that same desire to learn and grow, reading several books a month and saturating his life with the Word of God! He is an example of being a lifelong learner.

If you are going to disciple others, you must first be a disciple yourself, learning, growing, and following Jesus!

I have shared from the Word of God and from my experiences what I believe are the character qualities that must be cultivated in your life if you desire to be used by God as an effective disciplemaker. As we explore 2 Timothy 2 in the next chapters, my hope is for you to see several pictures of both the heart and character of a disciplemaker.

3

A Picture Is Worth a Thousand Words

Have you ever heard the expression, "A picture is worth a thousand words"? While visiting my wife's parents in Wyoming one summer, we had the opportunity to go to Yellowstone National Park. Yellowstone is breathtaking! There is no way to describe the beauty, wonder, and grandeur of Yellowstone with mere words.

The phrase "A picture is worth a thousand words" comes from an ancient Chinese proverb that says, "A picture paints a thousand characters." It means to say a picture or illustration can convey an idea or truth with a thousand times more clarity than words can.

When writing 2 Timothy, the apostle Paul knew he was coming to the end of his life and ministry, and he sent one final letter to Timothy, admonishing him to guard the gospel that had been entrusted to him. In chapter 2, Paul reminded Timothy of the qualities a godly leader must have. He painted a full-length portrait of what a disciplemaker ought to look like if he is to entrust the gospel to others.

According to 2 Timothy 2, to be a disciplemaker is to be above reproach. In the next three chapters, we'll discover that the disciplemaker ought to be the following:

- A steward entrusting the gospel to faithful men and women
- A soldier enduring hardship to please his or her commander
- An athlete who trains and competes according to the rules
- A farmer who works hard planting, watering, cultivating, and harvesting
- An approved worker who rightly divides the Word of God
- A vessel fit for the Master's use
- A bondservant desiring to please his or her Lord

[Handwritten annotations in top margin: "KDC = Paul-Spirken. New Face", "Busy - its jut an hour", "full ill equipped - train", "Culture -", "Weak place / What excites / passionate about", "+ Surrendered", "+ Expected - Must if have conv-", "+ cannot vision + leaders"]

Before we dive into this text, let me remind you of several things that are foundational. ~~[struck through handwriting]~~

First, Christ followers are not to be *consumers*; they are to be gospel *coworkers*. Regrettably, this is not the case in most churches. After surveying thousands of evangelical churches, Ed Stetzer lamented, "The majority of members in the majority of our churches are not engaged in meaningful ministry or missions."[xi]

Second, members ought to see themselves as ministers, not just members. Notice what Paul said in Ephesians chapter 4: "And He personally gave some to be apostles, some prophets, some evangelists, some pastors and teachers, for the training of the saints in the work of ministry, to build up the body of Christ, until we all reach unity in the faith and in the knowledge of God's Son, growing into a mature man with a stature measured by Christ's fullness" (Eph. 4:11–13).

The work of pastors and teachers is to train, or equip, others to do the work of ministry. They are not doing ministry alone; they are seeking to empower all their members to do ministry so the church body can grow and mature. The primary ministry of the local church is to make disciples who make disciples.

Third, ministry will occur when God works through you to meet the needs of others for His glory. Notice what Paul said in Ephesians 2: "For you are saved by grace through faith, and this is not from yourselves; it is God's gift—not from works, so that no one can boast. For we are His creation, created in Christ Jesus for good works, which God prepared ahead of time so that we should walk in them" (Eph. 2:8–10).

The word translated as "creation" in the HCSB is a word that means "masterpiece." This implies that God is actively involved in doing a deep work in you so He can work through you to accomplish His purposes!

As you read and reflect on these next three chapters, I want you to picture yourself not just as a church member but as a minister who makes disciples.

THE STEWARD

According to Paul, a disciplemaker is to be a faithful steward of Christ. A steward is one who manages the resources and the affairs of another. As a steward of

Christ, you will not manage material wealth; you will manage spiritual treasures. Paul wrote to Timothy, "You, therefore, my son, be strong in the grace that is in Christ Jesus. And what you have heard from me in the presence of many witnesses, commit to faithful men who will be able to teach others also" (2 Tim. 2:1–2).

As a steward of Christ, you must serve in the strength God supplies and invest in men and women of integrity.

Serve in the Strength God Supplies.

The steward of Christ does not serve in his own ability or power. Instead, he is wholly dependent on Christ and serves in the strength God supplies.

In John Stott's commentary on 2 Timothy, *Guard the Gospel*, he elaborates on this: "Timothy [or any disciplemaker] will not find strength for ministry in his own nature or ability, but in the grace that God supplies. The grace of God is not only for our salvation, it is for our service."[xii]

Consider also what Paul says in Colossians 1: "We proclaim Him, warning and teaching everyone with all wisdom, so that we may present everyone mature in Christ. I labor for this, striving with His strength that works powerfully in me" (Col. 1:28–29).

Paul is laboring and striving, but at the same time, he recognizes that the Lord Jesus is working powerfully through him as he submits and surrenders to the Christ within. Is it any wonder he says to the Corinthians that believers "are God's coworkers" (1 Cor. 3:9)?

Invest in Men and Women of Integrity.

"And what you have heard from me in the presence of many witnesses, commit to faithful men who will be able to teach others also" (2 Tim. 2:2).

Paul told Timothy, on more than one occasion, to guard the gospel. Robby Gallaty helps us understand what this means: "The way Timothy would guard the gospel entrusted to him would be by giving it away."[xiii]

By entrusting the gospel he'd received to faithful people, Timothy was ensuring it would continue to thrive among all people. Faithful men are men or women who are people of FAITH: they are faithful, available, intentional, teachable, and hungry.

Those you invest in should be faithful. People who are faithful will persevere and endure through hardships. They are steadfast in their commitments and hold true in spite of circumstances. These men and women have proven themselves trustworthy.

Second, those you invest in should be available. These are the folks that are always ready, willing, and able to do the work of God or to serve and minister to others.

Third, those you invest in should be intentional. They are not only ready, willing, and able to do God's work, but they are also searching for things to do. These are people who see opportunities for ministry and seize them for the glory of God.

Fourth, those you invest in should be teachable. Being teachable may be the most important character quality of someone you invest in. So many do not receive instruction because they think they've arrived and know it all.

Finally, those you invest in should be hungry. They should have a hunger and thirst for God. Like one who is hungry and thirsty, they are seeking God and will not be satisfied until they come to know Him in a deeper way. Jesus said, "Those who hunger and thirst for righteousness are blessed, for they will be filled" (Matt. 5:6).

While in seminary, I served as the student pastor at the First Baptist Church of Kennedale, Texas. The senior pastor, Earnest Wall, taught me a valuable lesson that I will never forget. He said, "If you are going to be in gospel ministry, you must see people not for who they are but for what they can become." That principle has served me well over the years working with students and adults alike.

Faithful stewards must begin with the end in mind. As they invest in men and women who are faithful, available, intentional, teachable, and hungry, they must see others for what they can become as Christ works in them.

Paul's desire was not to see converts but to help those who came to faith become mature and devoted followers of Christ. And that should be the heartfelt desire of every disciplemaker: to see people come to faith and be discipled.

The only way we can do this is by "His strength which works powerfully" in us (Col. 1:29). Paul knew that as he allowed Christ to work *in* him, Christ would work *through* him as he invested in others.

The steward of Christ must entrust the gospel to faithful men who can give it away to the next generation. In 2 Timothy 2:2, there are four generations mentioned:

First, Christ gave away the gospel to Paul.

Second, Paul gave it away to Timothy.

Then Timothy would entrust it to faithful men.

Finally, faithful men would then teach others also.

Paul equipped and empowered Timothy—who would then equip and empower faithful men—who would then equip and empower others also! In whom are you investing? Whom are you equipping and empowering to do gospel ministry?

I once heard the story of a congregational pastor who was visited by the bishop of his district. The bishop asked, "How many converts did you have in this last church year?"

"We had one young boy," the pastor replied proudly, "and I have been mentoring and investing in him to help him grow in his faith."

The bishop replied, "Only one convert to show for a year of gospel work; that is disgraceful."

But the pastor was not discouraged. He continued to pour into and invest in this young man. He helped him walk through the Bible, memorize Scripture, share his faith, and find a burden for prayer. God blessed this pastor's efforts; the young man grew up to become the powerful preacher F. B. Meyer.

As a disciplemaker, you have been entrusted with the spiritual treasure of the gospel. You can leave a lasting legacy if you invest what you have received in the lives of others and then empower them to do the same. You can change the world from right where you live when you make disciples who make disciples.

But a disciplemaker is not only to be a steward of Christ; he is to be a soldier of the cross.

THE SOLDIER

According to Paul, the disciplemaker is also a soldier. He continues in his letter to Timothy, "Share in suffering as a good soldier of Christ Jesus. No one serving as a soldier gets entangled in the concerns of civilian life; he seeks to please the recruiter" (2 Tim. 2:3–4).

John Stott gave clear insight: "Paul's imprisonments had given him ample opportunity to observe Roman soldiers, and to meditate on the parallels between a soldier and a disciplemaker."[xiv]

Consider several of these parallels from the texts:

"He endures suffering" (Stott). "Share in suffering as a good soldier of Christ Jesus" (2 Tim. 2:3).

Following Jesus is not an easy undertaking. It will be hard, lonely, and costly at times. In the same way a soldier must endure hardships, the disciplemaker must endure and persevere in trials and adversity for the sake of the gospel. It is not an easy thing; it will take every spiritual resource grace can offer.

"He avoids entanglements" (Stott). "No one serving as a soldier gets entangled in the concerns of civilian life; he seeks to please the recruiter" (2 Tim. 2:4).

The soldier is entirely committed to the one who enlisted him. His allegiance is unwavering and un-shakeable. He will not allow anyone or anything to distract him from being all in! In the same way, the disciplemaker is to have an unwavering allegiance and loyalty to Jesus Christ. He or she cannot allow anyone or anything to distract or deter him or her from a sure commitment to Christ.

"He looks upon Christ" (Stott). "Keep your attention on Jesus Christ as risen from the dead and de-scended from David. This is according to my gospel" (2 Tim. 2:8).

The disciplemaker is to keep his or her attention on Jesus Christ. The disciplemaker may glance at all that is around him or her, but the disciplemaker must fix his or her gaze upon Christ!

The writer of Hebrews said it this way: "Keeping our eyes on Jesus, the source and perfecter of our faith, who for the joy that lay before Him endured a cross and despised the shame and has sat down at the right hand of God's throne. For consider Him who endured such hostility from sinners against Himself, so that you won't grow weary and lose heart" (Heb. 12:2–3).

"He looks out for fellow soldiers" (Stott). "This is why I endure all things for the elect: so that they also may obtain salvation, which is in Christ Jesus, with eternal glory" (2 Tim. 2:10).

The disciplemaker who knows he is a soldier fixes his or her gaze on the Lord Jesus but also looks out for other soldiers engaged in warfare. He suffers and endures all things for those who are "the elect," those who have been saved, and those who have not yet put their faith in Christ.

Several years ago, I heard Grant Teaff, former football coach at Baylor, speak at a coach's clinic. He closed his talk by summarizing the "power of one" with this quote:

"I am only one, but I am one.

"I can't do everything, but I can do something.

"And that which I ought to do, by God's grace I will do!"

He then went on to say, "You be that one!"

That is my challenge to you: be that one. Be the kind of disciplemaker who is a faithful steward, who is totally dependent on God, and who relies on His resources as he invests in others. Be the kind of disciplemaker who has a soldier's "whatever it takes" attitude to accomplish the work of God. Everything a disciplemaker does is to please the One who called him or her.

4

Ministry That Costs Nothing
Accomplishes Nothing

When you consider the life of the apostle Paul, you will discover that he was not an armchair quarterback; he had some "skin" in the game. He was no stranger to investing in others or enduring hardships, to the point that he said, "This is why I endure all things for the elect" (2 Tim. 2:10). He decided he would do whatever it took to know Christ and to make Him known.

On one occasion, Paul was asked to produce some credentials regarding his apostleship. In 2 Corinthians 11, it was as if Paul said, "You want some credentials? I'll give you some." Paul was scourged five times; he was beaten with rods three times; he was stoned, shipwrecked, and stranded in all kinds of danger; and he was under constant stress caring for the many churches he helped to organize. He suffered for the sake of the gospel.

Yet, in spite of all he endured, Paul had a single-minded devotion to know Christ and to advance the gospel. "Now I want you to know, brothers, that what has happened to me has actually resulted in the advance of the gospel" (Phil. 1:12).

Timothy was no stranger to adversity either—he was young, inexperienced, and shy. He faced opposition, resistance, and persecution from so-called brothers. His church was plagued by false doctrine, which would lead to false deeds. Paul and Timothy knew this principle well! Ministry that costs nothing accomplishes nothing.

Throughout this chapter, I hope you realize that gospel ministry will require sacrifice, self-discipline, and hard work so you won't be easily discouraged or disillusioned when adversity comes your way. As we examine this passage, let's consider three more portraits of a disciplemaker.

THE ATHLETE

Paul compares the disciplemaker to an athlete, saying, "If anyone competes as an athlete, he is not crowned unless he competes according to the rules"

(2 Tim. 2:5).

The "athlete" in the language of the New Testament is "one who strives, or agonizes for mastery."

Paul had already instructed Timothy years before: "But have nothing to do with irreverent and silly myths. Rather, train yourself in godliness, for the training of the body has a limited benefit, but godliness is beneficial in every way, since it holds promise for the present life and also for the life to come"

(1 Tim. 4:7–8).

In the same way that an athlete disciplines himself or herself and trains for excellence in the games, Timothy had to "discipline himself" and "train" for the purpose of godliness.

Godly living should be one of the sterling qualities of a disciplemaker. Paul would tell the Philippian church leaders, "Live your life in a manner worthy of the gospel of Christ" (Phil. 1:27). The principle is clear: when you and I conduct ourselves in a manner worthy of the gospel, the gospel becomes more believable.

I came to faith at a student summer camp. The thing God used to impact my life and cause me to really examine the claims of Christ was not just what the students and their leaders said but how they lived their lives! When I saw Christ in them, it gave me a hunger to know the Christ they knew. It made the gospel attractive. As disciplemakers, we should strive to allow others to see Jesus in us, so they will be attracted to the Christ we serve.

Paul admonished Timothy to not only strive for excellence but also to compete according to the rules. If an athlete breaks the rules, he or she will be disqualified. Accordingly, if a disciplemaker breaks the rules, he or she will be disqualified from ministry and bring shame and reproach to his Lord.

John MacArthur offered a great insight: "Paul is actually telling Timothy, 'Timothy, look at ministry the same way an athlete looks at competition in the games. Play to win!'"[xv]

A disciplemaker plays to win by following biblical principles and by having accountability in his or her life.

If a believer wishes to be a godly example to those he or she mentors and disciples, it stands to reason that the disciplemaker must surrender to God and to His Word. This means that the disciplemaker must strive to live his or her life by the principles and precepts of the Word. The disciplemaker must saturate his or her life with the Word in order to have it on his or her mind moment by moment.

You can do this in six primary ways.

First, saturate your life with the Word of God by hearing it proclaimed. It is crucial to sit under the preaching of the gospel. Hearing someone rightly divide the Word of Truth each week provides nourishment to our souls.

Second, spend time in the Word. Having a systematic reading plan in place will help you become familiar with the metanarrative of Scripture and the whole counsel of God. In addition to reading, it is helpful to journal as you read. I would recommend the HEAR method of journaling and the Foundations (F-260) Bible-reading plan.

Third, study the Word. In addition to a daily, disciplined, systematic reading of the Word, I would recommend studying through the inductive method: observation, interpretation, and application.

Fourth, memorize the Word. The psalmist said in Psalm 119:11, "I have treasured Your word in my heart so that I may not sin against You." Fill your heart and mind with the Word by committing it to memory.

Fifth, meditate on the Word. You picture, ponder, and pray over a text of Scripture as you reflect upon it over and over again. The word picture for this principle in the Hebrew language is that of a dove cooing or a cow chewing the cud. Repeat it to yourself throughout the day so that it nourishes you all day long.

Finally, apply the Word. James said it well in James 1:22–25: "But be doers of the word and not hearers only, deceiving yourselves. Because if anyone is a hearer of the word and not a doer, he is like a man looking at his own face in a mirror. For he looks at himself, goes away, and immediately forgets what kind of man he was. But the one who looks intently into the perfect law of freedom and perseveres in it, and is not a forgetful hearer but one who does good works—this person will be blessed in what he does."

In addition to saturating his or her life with the Word, a disciplemaker should also practice accountability. Accountability, practically speaking, is being responsible for or answerable to someone else. *Accountable relationships can only happen when we give others the right to walk alongside us, observe our lives, and share those things that don't measure up to Christ.* All of us need accountability in our lives, especially those who make disciples.

I'll never forget the first time I heard Jeff play the saxophone. It was obvious he was a phenomenal musician. Jeff had gotten involved in our campus ministry at Nicholls State University and appeared to have everything going for him. He was good looking and really smart, and he could play almost any instrument. Jeff claimed to be a believer and seemed to be an awesome guy.

However, as we got better acquainted with Jeff, we discovered that he lacked discipline and was unable to finish almost anything he started. Because he only had surface relationships with the guys at the BCM and had no accountability in his life, he continually made poor decisions. As a result, his life was in danger of becoming a train wreck.

One of our students invited Jeff to be in a discipleship group that we at the time called a covenant group. It was the first time Jeff had welcomed any accountability in his life, and that was the difference that made the difference.

Because the other members of the group had permission to speak into his life, he came to a saving faith, was more disciplined in his commitments, and began to have meaningful relationships that centered on Christ and the gospel.

The disciplemaker is not only pictured as an athlete; he or she is also pictured as a farmer.

THE FARMER

"The hardworking farmer ought to be the first to get a share of the crops" (2 Tim. 2:6).

A disciplemaker is like a farmer: plowing, planting, watering, cultivating, and harvesting. But God gives the increase! This image reminds us of several principles that are true of farming as well as disciplemaking.

First, farming takes hard work.

Farmers get up before sunrise and usually work long after dark. Remember, gospel work is hard work!

During the summer of 1975, I had the opportunity to serve at Camp Rockmont for Boys in Black Mountain, North Carolina. It was one of the most challenging summers of my young life as a new believer in Christ. I had the responsibility of shepherding several young men who were twelve to fourteen years old. The days were long, and the work was hard, but it was so worth it because I saw lives change in these young men through the gospel.

That's the way it still is after all these years of investing in others. It's worth it because of the transformation you see in others as God works through you to meet the needs of those around you for His glory.

Next, farming takes patience.

"Therefore, brothers, be patient until the Lord's coming. See how the farmer waits for the precious fruit of the earth and is patient with it until it receives the early and the late rains" (James 5:7).

Those who are in gospel work must be patient because spiritual growth takes time. It is slow and tedious, so we must be patient to show and share the love of Christ by investing in the lives of others even when we don't see progress!

As Warren Wiersbe said, "Only Eternity will reveal the harvest God has accomplished through us."[xvi]

Farming yields a portion of the crop reserved for the farmer.

All disciplemakers get the privilege of enjoying their share of the "crop." Think of the joys of ministry: leading people to Christ, seeing lives changed and transformed, having rich fellowship with Christ, and cultivating life-long friendships.

When you think of ministry, don't think microwave; instead, think Crock-Pot! It requires hard work and patience, but there is joy unspeakable and full of glory!

While serving at the Nicholls State BCM, I had the opportunity to disciple a young man named Kevin who became a son in the faith to me, a great ministry partner, and a student leader on the campus.

As part of our discipleship pathway on campus, we started some discipleship groups. Kevin and I each had a group. My group was going well, and Kevin's group seemed to be losing traction. Derek and Tony (guys who were in Kevin's group) just weren't as faithful as the guys in my group. They weren't consistent with their assignments, seldom memorized Scripture, and failed to come to all the meetings.

One day, Kevin came into my office, upset. I asked him what was wrong, and he told me that he was going to stop meeting with the group. When I asked him why, he said, "You always get the good guys, and I always get the scrubs."

After I shared with Kevin that spiritual growth takes time and that we must be patient to allow God to work, he left my office with a resolve to patiently journey together with Derek and Tony. For the rest of that year, Kevin and I got to watch God work, seeing Derek and Tony changed and transformed by the power of God!

Fast-forward several years later, and Derek and Tony were leading one of our worship gatherings on campus. It became obvious that God had done a work in their lives. They led the gathering with excellence, preaching and leading in meaningful worship.

During the service, I noticed that Kevin was grinning from ear to ear, pleased by what he had seen and heard. After the service, knowing that Kevin was thrilled over his group of guys, I went up to him and said, "Not bad for a bunch of scrubs!"

The point is this: As disciplemakers, we must be as patient as a farmer who is trusting God for a spiritual harvest. We plant, water, and cultivate, but God is the one who always brings the growth.

The disciplemaker is to be a faithful steward, a suffering soldier, an athlete who strives to win the prize, and a hard-working farmer. But the disciplemaker is also to be an approved workman.

THE WORKER

"Be diligent to present yourself approved to God, a worker who doesn't need to be ashamed, correctly teaching the word of truth" (2 Tim. 2:15).

That word "worker" in the language of the New Testament is where we get the English word "craftsman." This word picture is especially for all those who handle the Word of God! Those who teach, equip, and train are to be skilled craftsmen when it comes to the Word!

John Stott elaborated on this passage by highlighting three insights:

1. Workers are here to teach.
2. There are two kinds of workers: those who are approved and those who are ashamed.

3. The difference between these two kinds of workers is how they handle the Word of God.[xvii]

Those who handle God's Word accurately will be approved and rewarded when they stand before Him. Conversely, those who do not handle the Word accurately will be ashamed when they stand before Him. The disciplemaker must strive to rightly divide the Word of Truth.

We believe disciplemaking means equipping believers with the Word of God through accountable relationships, empowered by the Holy Spirit, to replicate faithful followers of Christ. If that's true, we must handle the Word of God accurately and help those we disciple to do the same. Whenever I have the opportunity to speak into someone's life, I emphasize the importance of correctly handling Scripture.

Peter said it this way in 1 Peter 4:11: "If anyone speaks, it should be as one who speaks God's words; if anyone serves, it should be from the strength God provides, so that God may be glorified through Jesus

Christ in everything. To Him belong the glory and the power forever and ever. Amen."

When you invest in others, model by your manner of life and treatment of Scripture "correctly teaching the word of truth" (2 Tim. 2:15). Take advantage of those teachable moments to encourage the men and women you mentor to have a godly respect for the Word of God, to saturate their lives with it, to interpret it correctly, and to apply it to their lives.

5

A Vessel Fit for the Master's Use

More than anything else, I want to bring glory to God by being someone He can work through. There is an old chorus I heard many years ago, written by Audrey Mieir and sung by Andrae Crouch, that expresses my heart:

To be used of God,
To sing, to speak, to pray.
I long so much to feel the touch
Of God's consuming fire.
To be used of God
This is my desire.

Is it your desire to be used of God, to be someone He can work through to accomplish His purpose? *Ministry, at its very core, is allowing Christ to work through us to meet the needs of others for His glory!* To be "useful" is to be suitable for God to work through—a vessel fit for the Master's use.

This idea of usefulness is found in 2 Timothy 4:11: "Only Luke is with me. Bring Mark with you, for he is useful to me in the ministry." Those who are familiar with the backstory know that there was a time when Mark was not useful to Paul, but now he said of Mark, "He is useful to me."

Paul also used the same word translated as "useful" in Philemon: "Appeal to you for my son, Onesimus. I fathered him while I was in chains. Once he was useless to you, but now he is useful both to you and to me" (Philem. 1:10–11). There was a time when Onesimus was "not useful," but he became useful not only to Paul but to Philemon. I don't know about you, but I don't want to be useless to the Lord. I want to be useful—someone He can work in and through to accomplish His purposes.

In this chapter, I want to help you see what God requires so you can be a person He is pleased to use. As we examine this passage, notice two word pictures used to describe a disciplemaker.

THE VESSEL

The first word picture in this passage is that of a vessel. In fact, there are two kinds of vessels used in the great house—one for honorable use, one for dishonorable. The great house is a picture of the church. Notice what Paul says in verse 19: "Nevertheless, God's solid foundation stands firm, having this inscription: The Lord knows those who are His, and Everyone who names the name of the Lord must turn away from unrighteousness" (2 Tim. 2:19).

God's firm foundation is the church built upon the Lord Jesus Christ. *Disciplemakers should make disciples in the context of the local church, not separate and apart from it.* As disciplemakers, we want to teach those we invest in to love what Jesus loves. Jesus loves the church and gave Himself for it, so those we invest in should have a love for God and His church.

Also, notice the last part of the verse: "The Lord knows those who are His, and everyone who names the name of the Lord must turn away from unrighteousness" (2 Tim. 2:19b).

There is a God-centered focus as well as a man-centered focus in this passage. The God-centered focus says, "The Lord knows those who are His," and the man-centered focus says, "Everyone who names the name of the Lord must turn away from unrighteousness." This verse highlights the sovereignty of God and the responsibility of man; both are taught in the Bible!

Warren Wiersbe stated: "Those who are the elect of God, prove it by living a godly life."[xviii]

The great house not only has a solid foundation, but it also contains various household utensils. These utensils or vessels have different purposes. Some are honorable—those of gold or silver—and some are dishonorable—those of wood and clay. He is not making a distinction between believers and unbelievers; he is referring to those who are useful and those who are not.

In this context, Paul is admonishing Timothy to separate himself from false teachers because false doctrines lead to false deeds. Those who handle God's Word accurately are vessels of honor, whereas those who don't are vessels of dishonor. Those who handle the Word correctly are proudly displayed as vessels fit for use. These vessels can be used for eating and serving, but the vessels of dishonor are used for garbage.

So, Paul is telling Timothy to be an honorable vessel. But what does it mean to be an honorable vessel? Notice the description in verse 21: "So if anyone purifies himself from anything dishonorable, he will be a special instrument, set apart, useful to the Master, prepared for every good work" (2 Tim. 2:21).

The disciplemaker should be a special instrument, one who cleanses himself from what is dishonorable. He should be many things:

Set Apart
In a sense, this has already happened in the life of a believer. The moment he or she came to faith, he or she was "set apart." But Paul is not talking about a

believer's position in Christ; he is talking about one's practice.

To be set apart is to be reserved for holiness unto God. In other words, the disciplemaker strives to practice righteousness and not practice sin. He or she deals with sin and the self-life, putting it to death so that the Holy Spirit within can control and empower him or her to live a life pleasing to God.

When I first met Nick, he was far from God. Even though he professed Christ, he was not following Him and was engaging in activities other college students his age were doing.

Nick's dad prayed for him and almost tricked him into going to an Experiencing God weekend. During that weekend, God dealt with Nick and showed him that those who profess an authentic relationship with Christ prove it by living life under His lordship. They live up to the faith they profess to believe. Nick drove a spiritual stake down and purposed to turn from the things that were keeping him from being devoted to God and trusting God to make him the man He desired him to be.

In time, Nick grew in his faith and become one of the student leaders in our ministry. He, along with his wife, Tara, serve at a church in south Louisiana. He is a godly pastor and is intentional about investing and pouring into the lives of others.

I often pray that God will keep me clean and close—clean from the stain of sin and close to Him. This doesn't happen by accident. We must die to self and crown Jesus King over our lives. As we go hard after Him, we must put to death anything that doesn't bring Him glory and embrace those things that help cultivate a rich and growing relationship with God.

As Christ lives His life in and through the disciple-maker, he or she can love as Jesus loves, serve as Jesus serves, and live as Jesus lives in total dependence and surrender to the Father.

Useful to the Master

The useful servant of God is totally surrendered, both as an instrument God can work with and a vessel He can work through. He or she is submissive and obedient to the master of the house, who is a picture of Christ.

In the same way, a disciplemaker should be surrendered and obedient to the Spirit of God. His attitude and mind-set should be "Not my will, but yours, be done" (Luke 22:42b). *After all, those you invest in are not really your disciples; they are disciples of Christ.* When we model surrender and obedience to the will and purpose of God, we are not only useful to Him but are great examples for those we disciple.

As Robby Gallaty often says to those who make disciples, "You can't expect what you don't emulate."[xix]

According to Jesus (Luke 14:26–33), three things will keep you from being fully devoted to God: other people, your priorities, and material possessions. These things will attract us and at the same time distract our attention from godly devotion.

In Luke 14:26, Jesus warned us about people. Notice what He said: "If anyone comes to Me and does not hate his own father and mother, wife and children, brothers and sisters—yes, and even his own life—he cannot be My disciple."

In the language of the New Testament, to "hate" means to "love less." To be the kind of man or woman who is useful to the Master, we must love God supremely. To be His disciple, we must love Him more than anyone else.

Jesus not only talked about our relationships with people, but He also talked about our priorities. Our priorities can keep us from being useful to the Master. Jesus said in verse 27, "Whoever does not bear his own cross and come after Me cannot be My disciple."

When Jesus said that we are to bear our own crosses and come after Him, He was saying we are to identify with Him completely. In other words, we are to make our relationship with Him our first priority. When we make Him our first priority, all other priorities should fall into place.

Jesus also said that our material possessions can keep us from being His disciples, from being people who are useful to the Master. He continued in verse 33, "In the same way, therefore, every one of you who does not say good-bye to all his possessions cannot be My disciple" (Luke 14:33).

Jesus knew that our material possessions could preoccupy our minds and keep us from being fully devoted to Him.

Prepared for Every Good Work

The idea here is that the vessel that God can work through is available. This person is ready and willing to serve. I like what Henry Blackaby said: "God is not so much concerned with your ability as He is about your availability." He went on to say, "Many believers are not useful to God because they hold on to sin. They are not submissive or obedient to God, and they are reluctant to do anything for Him!"[xx]

Cynthia came to the campus from Houston, Texas, on a volleyball scholarship. She was a great student and a gifted student athlete, and she had a heart for God and His Word. She became involved in the BCM as soon as she arrived on campus, and it was obvious that she was an amazing young woman.

It wasn't long before Cynthia became one of our student leaders. Her availability to God highlighted her life and ministry. She was always willing to invest and pour into the lives of her teammates and others on campus. In fact, while she was a student leader in our ministry, she led many to Christ and then discipled them so they could grow spiritually. Cynthia and her husband, Byron, serve the Lord today in south Louisiana. She is a gifted counselor, and he pastors a local church in Baton Rouge.

Is that you? Do you want to be useful to God?

We've seen that some are useful to God while others are not—they are more concerned about themselves. So, what must you do to be the kind of person God can use? Here are two directives from the text.

You must pursue a pure fellowship.

Notice the phrase in verse 21: "Purifies himself from anything dishonorable." In this context, Timothy was to separate himself from false teaching, from those who perverted the gospel of grace. But there is a greater application here—if you want to be the kind of person God can use, separate yourself from anything or anyone who would defile you.

Sin spreads like gangrene. This is the clear teaching of Scripture. Here are just a few examples:

"How happy is the man who does not follow the advice of the wicked or take the path of sinners or join a group of mockers! Instead, his delight is in the Lord's instruction, and he meditates on it day and night. He is like a tree planted beside streams of water that bears its fruit in season and whose leaf does not wither. Whatever he does prospers" (Ps. 1:1–3).

"I wrote to you in a letter not to associate with sexually immoral people. I did not mean the immoral people of this world" (1 Cor. 5:9–10a).

"But now I am writing you not to associate with anyone who claims to be a believer who is sexually immoral or greedy, an idolater or verbally abusive, a drunkard or a swindler. Do not even eat with such a person" (1 Cor. 5:11).

"Bad company corrupts good morals" (1 Cor. 15:33).

If you want to be the kind of person God can use, you must not only pursue a pure fellowship—you must pursue a pure heart.

You must pursue a pure heart.

"Flee from youthful passions, and pursue righteousness, faith, love, and peace, along with those who call on the Lord from a pure heart" (2 Tim. 2:22).

John MacArthur wrote, "If one would be useful to God, he must be a kind of 'running man.' He must 'run away' from youthful lusts and he must 'run to' righteousness!"[xxi]

Paul admonished the disciplemaker to flee from youthful passions and pursue godly character. This passage in 2 Timothy reminds us of the fruit of the Spirit mentioned in Galatians 5:22–23, which said, "But the fruit of the Spirit is love, joy, peace, patience, kindness, goodness, faith, gentleness, self-control. Against such things there is no law."

The disciplemaker is portrayed not only as a vessel but also as a slave.

THE SLAVE

"But reject foolish and ignorant disputes, knowing that they breed quarrels. The Lord's slave must not quarrel, but must be gentle to everyone, able to teach, and patient, instructing his opponents with gentleness. Perhaps God will grant them repentance leading them to the knowledge of the truth. Then they may come to their senses and escape the Devil's trap, having been captured by him to do his will" (2 Tim. 2:23–26).

The second word picture in our text comes from the Greek word *doulos*, and it is translated as "slave" or "bondservant." So many in the Scriptures viewed themselves as servants or bondservants of God: Peter, James, John, Jude, and Paul, to name a few.

This is an incredible picture of what it means to be a disciplemaker. As a slave, you are identified with the person of your master, are obedient to the purposes of your master, and serve in the power and at the pleasure of your master. This portrays a total allegiance and dependence on Jesus Christ.

Paul shares that several things should be true of the Lord's slave or bondservant:

Not Quarrelsome

It is apparent from 2 Timothy 2:23 that these believers were engaged in arguments that would accomplish nothing. Paul began by saying that "the Lord's servant" must not become involved in these trivial disputes; they were foolish and fruitless! It is my experience that those who quarrel with others and are involved in meaningless arguments do not have a teachable spirit. My advice is that you shouldn't waste your time investing in those who have proven to be unteachable.

This doesn't mean that they can't ever disagree or push back, but it does mean that if they don't receive godly insight or instruction, you should find someone else to pour your life into.

Gentle to Everyone

The disciplemaker, according to Paul, should be gracious and kind to others. Consider what the Scriptures say in 1 Thessalonians 2:7–8: "Although we could have been a burden as Christ's apostles, instead we were gentle among you, as a nursing mother nurtures her own children. We cared so much for you that we were pleased to share with you not only the gospel of God but also our own lives, because you had become dear to us."

Able to Teach

The disciplemaker must not only be kind but must also be able to teach. This means that he or she should be effective when communicating the Word of God.

This does not mean that every disciplemaker needs to have the spiritual gift of teaching. Although you can be a disciplemaker without having the gift of teaching, you ought to strive to rightly divide the Word of God and become better at communicating the precepts and principles of the Scriptures.

Instructs with Gentleness

One of the principles of Scripture is that our manner of life is as important as what we say. In other words, our manner of life ought to match our speech.

As a disciplemaker, you will interact with people you will have to correct or instruct. When doing so, it is so important to instruct them with a spirit of humility and patience.

The disciple of Christ should be a growing follower of Jesus who is learning and applying the Word of

God, which leads to greater intimacy with Him and results in life change.

A disciplemaker must continue to learn more about who God is and also grow in godly character as he or she invests in others. A disciplemaker should see himself or herself as a bondservant of God, useful to the master, the Lord Jesus Christ!

6

Mentoring Emerging Leaders

One of the greatest privileges someone can have is to disciple or mentor emerging leaders who feel they've been called to vocational ministry. And yet, few pastors and church leaders take advantage of that wonderful opportunity.

When people share that God is dealing with them about a call to vocational ministry, we normally say to ourselves, "These individuals are feeling called to ministry, so I'll send them off to seminary." This is unfortunate because according to Barna Research, only 17 percent of evangelicals have had a godly mentor in their lives.[xxii] This thinking is neither biblical nor practical.

I have a strong conviction that it is the responsibility of leaders in the local church to disciple and mentor those called to vocational ministry. After they have affirmed God's calling, they can then go to seminary for specialized training, but higher education should not replace the valuable relationship between a mentor and a mentee.

So many practical things can be experienced by emerging leaders in the local church as they are discipled and mentored by their local church leaders. This is invaluable preparation and training that you can't reproduce in a classroom setting.

A mentor, by definition, is a trusted counselor, a guide, a tutor, or a coach. I'm so thankful that over the years, God has placed mentors in my life and has given me the great privilege of investing in scores of emerging leaders.[xxiii]

Here are several qualities of a godly mentor:

MODEL GODLY BEHAVIOR

The greatest gift you could give to emerging leaders in the church, especially to those who may be called to vocational ministry, is to live a godly life before them.

Peter told fellow elders and shepherds to be godly examples in 1 Peter 5:2–4: "Shepherd God's flock among you, not overseeing out of compulsion but freely, according to God's will; not for the money but eagerly; not lording it over those entrusted to you, but being examples to the flock. And when the chief Shepherd appears, you will receive the unfading crown of glory."

Paul admonished the church at Philippi to follow his example: "Do what you have learned and received and heard and seen in me, and the God of peace will be with you" (Phil. 4:9).

You must begin by modeling a godly life before your disciples. They are looking for someone to give them direction and to model what a godly man or woman looks like in everyday life. They're looking for someone who can flesh out the faith by applying scriptural principles to real-life situations.

This is especially true when things aren't going well. How we react in times of crisis and in difficult situations reveals our true characters. Do you respond by getting anxious and falling apart, or do you respond by trusting and depending on God?

While we were traveling across Texas to Mexico for a collegiate mission trip, our van broke down. Because it was a holiday weekend, we had a small window of time to act in securing transportation for part of our group. Rather than falling apart and thinking the trip was over, our student leaders asked the group to pray, secured a rental van, and had us on our way in a short time. They modeled what trusting God in the midst of a difficult situation looked like and taught our students more in their godly response than we could have taught them in a year of Bible studies.

ENCOURAGE AND AFFIRM

Be a cheerleader to those you mentor. We have more than enough naysayers and critics in our lives, so be someone who encourages and affirms!

Be intentional about affirming the good in your mentees' lives. Acknowledge and affirm godly character, attitudes, and actions. Look for ways to build them up and not tear them down. The author of Hebrews said, "And let us be concerned about one another in order to promote love and good works, not staying away from our worship meetings, as some habitually do, but encouraging each other, and all the more as you see the day drawing near" (Heb. 10:24–25).

Here are some practical action steps you can take to encourage and affirm:

Applaud Even the Little Steps of Growth.

Begin to speak into the lives of those you mentor, applauding even the smallest steps of growth you see displayed in their lives. Look for progress, and take the time to say something affirming for their good work, ideas, or meeting of specific goals and objectives.

If language changes cultures and words impact worlds, then words of encouragement and affirmation can help move someone from good to great!

Be Supportive and Optimistic.

Let your disciples or mentees know that you are on their team, that you love and support them, and that you want them to grow and succeed. Never get tired of telling them that you believe in them and their calling.

Help them to understand that God doesn't call the equipped; He equips the called. If God has called them to be leaders, He will give them all the resources needed to accomplish what He's called them to do. That includes helping them grow and develop as they depend upon Him.

Chip came to faith as an older teenager. He participated in our collegiate ministry while he was still in high school. Although Chip's relationship with Christ was rich and growing, he came from a broken home and struggled with a lack of confidence.

As we walked together, I began to help him understand that he was "accepted in the beloved" through Christ and that he had an amazing identity in Him. As the years went by, Chip grew to be a strong believer and disciplemaker, investing in and mentoring many emerging leaders.

Chip has a growing business in south Louisiana and is a bivocational pastor who is leading his church to make disciples who make disciples.

NEVER CEASE PRAYING

When you pray for those you disciple and mentor, you are trusting God for a couple of things.

First, when you pray, you are trusting God to do what only He can do. As Paul said in 1 Corinthians 3:6–7, "I planted, Apollos watered, but God gave the growth. So then neither the one who plants nor the one who waters is anything, but only God who gives the growth." *When you pray, you are believing that only God can grow a disciple of Christ.*

Second, when you pray, you are trusting God to help your disciple or mentee pursue Him.

If the late Jerry Bridges was correct in saying, "Sanctification is a work that God does that requires our effort," then it stands to reason that you should pray that your disciple or mentee should have a heart to pursue God. You should pray often that God will awaken godly affections and a desire to know Christ in a deep, intimate way.

Pray and model prayer often with your disciples. Since prayer is caught as much as it is taught, you should pray often with your disciples or mentees. Show them that you are dependent on God and not yourself, and help them learn that prayer is a never-ending conversation with God. The Lord Jesus and the apostle Paul modeled prayer for their disciples. You should do the same!

TAKE ADVANTAGE OF TEACHABLE MOMENTS

Most of the time, the thing that separates great mentors from mediocre ones is that great mentors take the initiative of walking through the open doors of opportunity. See those teachable moments, and take the initiative to share a word fitly spoken.

Spend Time with Your Disciples.

You will never earn the right or have the opportunity to share a timely word with your disciples or mentees unless you spend time with them. Notice what Paul said in 1 Thessalonians 2:8: "We cared so much for you that we were pleased to share with you not only the gospel of God but also our own lives because you had become dear to us."

When you share your life with others, it will cost you. You will have to set aside your own agenda and live intentionally for your mentee. As Paul wrote to the church at Philippi, "Do nothing out of rivalry or conceit, but in humility consider others as more important than yourselves. Everyone should look out not only for his own interests, but also for the interests of others" (Phil. 2:3–4).

Look for Teachable Moments.

When you spend quality time with your mentees or disciples, it is important to look for teachable moments where God can use you to share a principle or truth when they are able to receive it.

When your mentees ask a question looking for an easy answer, you can respond with, "That's a great question. What do you think?" It's okay to leave your mentees hanging for a time without being quick to answer, letting them struggle with a question or a paradox.

This was one of Jesus's chief teaching methods. He would frequently answer a question with a question.

Notice His interaction with His disciples from Matthew 16: "When Jesus came to the region of Caesarea Philippi, He asked His disciples, 'Who do people say that the Son of Man is?' And they said, 'Some say John the Baptist; others, Elijah; still others, Jeremiah or one of the prophets.' 'But you,' He asked them, 'who do you say that I am?' Simon Peter answered, 'You are the Messiah, the Son of the living God!' And Jesus responded, 'Simon son of Jonah, you are blessed because flesh and blood did not reveal this to you, but My Father in heaven'" (Matt. 16:13–17).

Jesus asked a question and let His disciples think about it and answer. But notice how Jesus responded to their answer with another more direct question in verse 15: "But who do you say that I am?" Jesus didn't let them repeat whatever the crowds were saying; He was asking them what they believed.

OFFER GODLY COUNSEL AND ACCOUNTABILITY

You should strive to help your disciples or mentees see things from God's viewpoint and not a human perspective—to see things through the lens of the Word of God and not by the wisdom of the world.

When offering godly counsel, base your counsel on the Word of God! Help your disciples or mentees to see principles that apply in the gray areas that Scripture has not specifically addressed, including answers to questions like these:

- "Whom should I marry?"
- "Is it wrong to smoke or drink?"
- "Should I move to this city or another?"

Also, you should offer accountability to those you disciple or mentor. You must hold those you disciple for God's agenda in their lives and not to your own.

We all need someone in our lives who loves us well! We need someone who will ask the tough questions to hold us accountable for growth and ministry development and performance.

In a growing, healthy, gospel-centered relationship, this accountability should never be abused, yet the truth remains, "We can't expect what we don't inspect."

First, this kind of relationship must be kingdom focused! The goal is to reach God's goal for growth and ministry, not the mentor's or disciplemaker's.

Second, the relationship should be voluntary. It is based on freedom in Christ, not some legalistic rule. In this relationship, there is no room for control, manipulation, or coercion.

Third, this relationship should be flexible. Any healthy relationship must grow over time. This relationship should not be rigid, but it should leave room for adjustment and change.

BE READY TO ASK DEEP QUESTIONS

A godly mentor should ask deep questions. A deep question is one that requires more than a simple yes or no answer. It is a question that requires thought and reflection. Skilled mentors tend to ask question after question to help those whom they disciple or mentor to arrive at the answer for themselves.

In addition to asking deep questions, skilled mentors listen well. They listen to what is said and what is not said. They "hear between the lines" so that their understanding is deepened and the mentoring relationship can grow.

SHARE SPIRITUAL INSIGHTS

Godly mentors and disciplemakers not only model lives that are consistent with the gospel, but they also share spiritual principles and insights. They take advantage of those teachable moments we talked about, and they share their faith in a systematic way. These should include things like the following:

Relationship with God

Godly mentors should model a rich and growing relationship with the Father as well as share meaningful spiritual insights that would help their mentees grow in their walks with God. Share things like helpful spiritual disciplines, scriptural precepts, and principles for spiritual growth.

Don't be afraid to share spiritual markers and real-life situations about how God worked to grow you and help you become more dependent on Him.

Servant Leadership

Another thing you should share with your mentee is the idea of servant leadership. A call to ministry is a call to lead the way Jesus did, as a servant! "For even the Son of Man did not come to be served, but to serve, and to give His life—a ransom for many" (Mark 10:45).

Discovering Spiritual Gifts

Help your mentees discover and use their spiritual gifts, especially those motivational gifts that will fuel their ministries. You can help them discover their spiritual gifts by using a spiritual gifts inventory and observing them as they serve and minister. When you recognize a particular gifting, encourage and talk to them about it. Be careful to ask deep questions and listen to their responses. Help them celebrate as they sense what God is doing in their lives.

Practical Ministry Skill Development

Give those you disciple opportunities to do some things they can use as they mature and develop—things like preparing and delivering a sermon or devotion, making a hospital visit, or leading one of the ordinances by officiating the Lord's Supper or baptism.

When doing this, follow the model Jesus used from Scriptures:

- Jesus did it, and the disciples watched.
- Jesus did it, and the disciples assisted.
- The disciples did it, and Jesus assisted.
- The disciples did it, and Jesus watched.

It is important to model the role before your mentees so they don't just hear what to do but can see what to do. Imitation may be a high form of flattery, but it is also a crucial part of learning how to live a godly life.

So What Now?

As you've now read in this book about the heart and qualities of a disciplemaker, my prayer is that you will take what you've learned and put it into practice. Don't just let this be something you read and then put away on a bookshelf; I hope you will intentionally decide to invest in the lives of others through gospel-centered relationships. Take some time to pray about who God would have you invest in, and seek out those opportunities. Don't miss the blessing of pouring your life into someone!

Let me leave you with the words of our Lord Jesus to both challenge and encourage you: "Then Jesus came near and said to them, "All authority has been given to Me in heaven and on earth. Go, therefore, and make disciples of all nations, baptizing them in the name of the Father and of the Son and of the Holy Spirit, teaching them to observe everything I have commanded you. And remember, I am with you always, to the end of the age" (Matt. 28:18–20).

Replicate Ministries exists to equip the local church to make disciples who make disciplemakers. We would love to help you as you follow Jesus's command to make disciples. Visit www.replicate.org for more information and free resources.

The Growing Up Series

01. GROWING UP: HOW TO BE A DISCIPLE WHO MAKES DISCIPLES

I think I'm a lot like you. There was a time in my life when I wanted to grow in my faith but just didn't know how.

- I owned a Bible but didn't understand it.
- I heard others pray but didn't know how to communicate with God.
- I wanted to share my faith with others but didn't know where to start.
- I had friends at church but lacked deep relationships with anyone.
- I wanted to hide God's Word in my heart but lacked a plan for memorization.
- I read the Scriptures but didn't know how to apply them.

Maybe this is where you are today. One day my life changed forever. What was the turning point? *I realized the importance and power of discipleship.*

Two men took the time to invest in my life: David Platt—author of *Radical* and *Follow Me*, as well as the foreword of my book—and Tim LaFleur. Since then, I have read nearly every book on discipleship, searching for answers to my questions.

Now I want to share my findings with you. *Growing Up* takes the guesswork out of growing closer to the Lord and equipping others to do the same. This book has the potential to change your life!

02. FIRMLY PLANTED: A BLUEPRINT FOR CULTIVATING A FORTIFIED FAITH

Why is spiritual growth so complicated?

Are you one of the many Christians desiring a closer relationship with God but having no idea where to begin? Then this book is for you! In biblical, practical, and simple terms, Robby Gallaty shares a road map for spiritual maturity. The book addresses topics such as these:

- How you can be sure of your salvation
- Why your identity in Christ affects everything you do

- How to overcome the three enemies that cripple a Christian's growth
- A battle plan for gaining victory over temptation
- The indispensable spiritual discipline every believer must foster

03. BEARING FRUIT: WHAT HAPPENS WHEN GOD'S PEOPLE GROW

Bearing Fruit is the third book in the *Growing Up* series. In this book, we will look at how God grows believers. We'll discuss how Christians can know they are saved, overcome temptation, as well as look at spiritual warfare from an internal and external perspective. *Bearing Fruit* is applicable for new and mature believers alike. Don't miss it. Be sure to follow replicate.org for all the latest information. Coming fall 2017.

CUSTOMIZED EQUIPPING

Every church wants to obey Jesus's command to make disciples.

Often, we find our ministry is geared to get as many people in the front door of our church as possible. The challenge is that people are leaving through the back door of the church just as quickly as they enter the front. We need to grow our people beyond simply being inviters to being investors. We teach them to share their faith, but they need to learn to share their lives.

"Jesus devoted 90 percent of his time to discipling twelve men" (Robby Gallaty).

Jesus used a radically different approach than what we see in the church today. We devote so much of our time to evangelistic strategies that we often neglect discipleship. Disciplemaking is both evangelism *and* discipleship. We need to show our people that Jesus didn't just save them *from* something (evangelism) but *for* something (discipleship). We must focus on both. We need a strategy founded on biblical principles that is practical and reproducible.

Imagine seeing a multiplying, disciplemaking movement ignite in your church or ministry.

Discipleship isn't a class you take, a program you attend, or a book you study; discipleship is the course of your life. Learn a tried-and-tested process for multiplying disciples in your ministry context. Our team can help you launch a disciplemaking movement in your church or ministry.

To connect with the Replicate Team about training in your context, go to replicate.org, or e-mail info@ replicate.org.

THE DISCIPLESHIP BLUEPRINT

The disciplemaking blueprint is a two-day experience that allows you to spend time in the context of a local church actively engaging in discipleship. You'll have the opportunity to spend time with staff as well as walk alongside members as you do the following:

1. Learn how to plan, formulate, and develop a disciplemaking culture in your church and its ministries (missions, women, and men)
2. Study Jesus's and other historical models for making disciples
3. Develop a comprehensive plan for raising up leaders in your church
4. Learn how to navigate issues that arise in your D-groups

5. Participate in a D-group led by an experienced disciplemaker
6. Consider principles and strategies for starting D-groups and multiplying mature believers in your context when you return

End Notes

i.   D. A. Carson, *Love in Hard Places* (Wheaton, IL: Crossway, 2002), 61.

ii.   Dietrich Bonhoeffer, *Life Together: The Classic Exploration of Life and Community*, trans. J. W. Doberstein (1937; San Francisco: HarperSanFrancisco, 1993), 110.

iii.   J. Oswald Sanders, *The Joy of Following Jesus* (Chicago, IL: Moody Press, 1990), 50.

iv.   Lynn Anderson, *They Smell Like Sheep: Biblical Leadership for the Twenty-First Century* (West Monroe, LA: Howard Publishing Company, 1997).

v.   Pete Charpentier, *Reaching the Next Level* (Castle Rock, CO: Cross Link Publishing, 2010), 18.

vi.   Warren W. Wiersbe, *The Bible Exposition Commentary, Vol. 2* (Wheaton, IL: Scripture Press, 1989), 169.

vii. Christopher B. Adsit, *Personal Disciplemaking: A Step-By-Step Guide for Leading a Christian from New Birth to Maturity* (Orlando, FL: Campus Crusade for Christ, 1996).

viii. Allegedly attributed to Theodore Roosevelt, but used frequently by John Maxwell, including in *Winning with People: Discover the People Principles That Work for You Every Time* (Nashville, TN: Thomas Nelson, 2004), 91.

ix. Edward McKenree Bounds, *Power through Prayer* (Harrisburg, PA: Trinity Press International, 2012).

x. Miles J. Stanford, *The Green Letters: Principles of Spiritual Growth* (Grand Rapids, MI: Zondervan Publishing House, 1975), 14.

xi. Ed Stetzer, *Breaking the Missional Code: Your Church Can Become a Missionary in Your Community* (Nashville, TN: Broadman and Holman Academic Publisher, 2006).

xii. John R. W. Stott, *Guard the Gospel: The Message of Second Timothy* (Downers Grove, IL: InterVarsity Press, 1973), 49–50.

xiii. Robby Gallaty, *Unashamed: Taking a Radical Stand for Christ* (Chattanooga, TN: AMG Exposition, 2010), 64.

xiv. John R. W. Stott, *Guard the Gospel: The Message of Second Timothy* (Downers Grove, IL: InterVarsity Press, 1973), 52.

xv. John F. MacArthur, *The MacArthur New Testament Commentary: Second Timothy* (Chicago, IL: Moody Bible Institute, 1995), 46.

xvi. Warren W. Wiersbe, *The Bible Exposition Commentary, Vol. 2* (Wheaton, IL: Scripture Press, 1989), 378.

xvii. John R. W. Stott, *Guard the Gospel: The Message of Second Timothy* (Downers Grove, IL: InterVarsity Press, 1973), 66.

xviii. Warren W. Wiersbe, *The Bible Exposition Commentary, Vol. 2* (Wheaton, IL: Scripture Press, 1989), 247.

xix. Robby Gallaty, *MARCS of a Disciple: A Biblical Guide for Gauging Spiritual Growth* (Hendersonville, TN: Replicate Resources, 2016).

xx. Henry Blackaby, *Experiencing God* (Nashville, TN: Lifeway Press, 2007).

xxi.   John F. MacArthur, *The MacArthur New Testament Commentary: Second Timothy* (Chicago, IL: Moody Bible Institute, 1995), 92.

xxii.   Barna Research, https://www.barna.com/research/new-research-on-the-state-of-discipleship/. Accessed online, January 11, 2017.

xxiii.   Definition of "mentor" from *Merriam-Webster's Dictionary*, https://www.merriam-webster.com/dictionary/mentor. Accessed online, January 11, 2017.